The Girl in the Void

A BOOK OF POEMS

SAMANTHA BUTTERFIELD

ISBN: 979-8-9999886-0-7

 Formatted with Vellum

To those sitting in darkness

May you find a light.

Contents

Hello   ix

Welcome to the Void   1
The Final Chance   3
I Want Hope   5
What I Wouldn't Do   7
The Lie   9
My Inner Child   11
Became Doomed   13
Belly Aches   15
Depression is an Infliction   17
Feels Like   19
Cursed   21
Worse   23
Bitter Irony   25
Light vs Dark   27
Undone   29
Immortal   31
My Aymosphere   33
My Mind is Condemned   35
My Heart is Broken   37
My Body is Haunted   39
Not Made for this World   41
Perpetual Darkness   43
Into the Unknown   45
Future Raincloud   47
Dust Storm   49
Fake Alibi   51
Never Whole   53
Please Don't   55
How...?   57
I Am It   59
Accidental Overdose   61

You're Too Late   63

I Sit   65

Weak   67

A Life of Waste   69

Time Doesn't Heal All Things   71

My Fate is Depressing   73

Pandora's Box of Death   75

Self Destroyed   77

Like Sand Through the Hourglass...   79

A Mistake Was Made   81

Little Monster   83

I Have a Debt to Pay   85

Always Read the Fine Print   87

Earth is Calling   89

Death Knows Me   91

Waltz With The Devil   93

Defeated   95

Succumb   97

Field of Tragedy   99

All Too Slowly   101

I Hate It Here   103

The Well   105

The Void   107

Who's Really to Blame?   109

But Myself   111

The Problem Increases   113

The Weight is Crushing   115

Here Lies the Questions   117

Never Getting Better   119

Scarred   121

Broken Girl   123

Soul of Theseus   125

The Girl in the Void   127

The Well Dried Up   129

Fathoms Deep   131

Not Through   133

Enough   135

Anymore   137

A Cycle of Darkness   139

A Plague   141

Slipping into Insanity   143

You Just Lost the Game   145

The Ugliest House on the Street   147

Dead   149

My World Ends   151

Well Traveled   153

I Suppose This Is It   155

You Could Not   157

Bad at Goodbyes   159

Their Grief Will Be Temporary   161

Sorry   163

Doomsday Clock   165

It All Ends   167

Grieving   169

A Last Parting   171

Goodbye   173

After Thought   175

Thank You   177

About the Author   179

Also by Samantha Butterfield   181

HELLO

I am constantly falling into **the void.**

The truth is once you go in you never fully come back up. You may linger closer to the top. Maybe a limb or the top of your head will poke out, but you are never free from it.

The void in my case is depression.

For you it may be something else. Perhaps it is addiction. Or grief. Or some other sort of madness.

Either way.... you chose this book for a reason.

Regardless of your motive or reasoning for picking this book up, **please read with caution.**

Stop and ask yourself...

Are you willing to sink deeper into your **void**?

If the answer is **no**, put this book down, get help and stay sane.

If the answer is yes well then....

WELCOME TO THE VOID

Time is irrelevant here
Seconds don't count
Minutes don't matter

Love is not enough here
Laughter is silent
Smiles don't exist

Life freezes in here
Hearts both stall and pump
Blood pours indefinitely

Death won't come here
An endless limbo
No peace and quiet

I can't escape here
No way to get out
Only deeper to go

THE FINAL CHANCE

I don't think it's ever felt like this before
The darkness in the horizon just taunts me
As I try to embrace life one last time
Another failure will kill me, but no one knows that
I'm holding in for dear life
Chasing every high I can
Just trying to dig my heels into the dirt
Before my body sinks too far down
Gravity is calling me from six feet down
But I resist with all my might
Knowing I'm running out of time
To find a reason to keep going
The end is nearer than ever before
Reaching for the stars just holding dust
Because it's never felt like this before
And I'm scared this is my last chance
I don't know if I'll survive this

I WANT HOPE

I inhale and for a moment
I believe I can do this
One good day and I find it
The faith I needed
But night always comes
And I always slip back into it
I can't escape the misery
But I want to

I smile and for a second
It feels real enough to last
One brief minute of no pain
Maybe I'm finally free
But the hurt always returns
And I always let it consume me
I can't avoid the suffering
But I want to

I break and for a once
I just want to be okay
One last attempt, please
Just let this be the end
But I'm always unlucky
And I always survive it
I can't end my existence
But I want to

WHAT I WOULDN'T DO

What I wouldn't do to rewind
Starting over could fix everything
Unless we want to finally accept
I was born defective
But we aren't, are we?

What I wouldn't do to stop this
One good day could fix it all
Unless we want to accept the truth
I don't have a chance left
But we aren't ready yet, are we?

What I wouldn't do to survive
No one could fix me
Unless we want to admit
I didn't let them
But we won't say that, will we?

What I wouldn't do to be better
Lessening the pain could change me
Unless we are ready to give up
I know I am done trying
But we can't let me, can we?

THE LIE

I don't want to die
And that's a lie
That I try to make true
But I can't make it real

I don't want to die
And I really do try
To keep ignoring it
But I can't stop

I don't want to die
And I hate saying it
Cause you believe me
But I wish you didn't

I don't want to die
And I fake it well enough
The truth buried deep
But it's a false screen

I don't want to die
And it's too late
To admit it
I do want to die

MY INNER CHILD

I walk the halls of the past
Feel the memories haunting me
A ghost over my shoulder
Reminding me all I was
The good and bad blend together
Mistakes rank high
And triumphs few and far between
For I took on the broken crown
Of the girl I should've been
Like a noose, I tied it around my neck
And not a day goes by where I don't remember
The fact I had a chance before crumbling
So as I dance in the grand ballroom
Of all my failed attempts of happiness
I waltz to the sounds of countless tears
And the numerous ways I tried to end it
Are piled in a corner keeping score
As I perform for the spirit of the girl I let down
And one day my tomb will bare her name
But it won't be her corpse there
Because she is rotting away
In the mansion of my mind
With the memories I still can't stand to recall
My inner child is a corpse of lost innocence

BECAME DOOMED

A horrible choice was made
A disaster happened
We all turned a blind eye
Pretended it wasn't happening
Hiding with our eyes shut tightly
Because facing the facts hurt worse
And no one had the answers
So it was best not to question it
Just let my soul shatter
Just let my fate sink faster
Because somehow
I became doomed
To lose

BELLY ACHES

The loneliest conversation starts in my gut
A rumble of grief and regret starts to spread
Word I never said are stuck in my throat
Phrases and jokes spill out instead
Because I'll never let the world know
All the horrible things I tell myself
That's a table for only me and myself
A conversation only I get to have
They would all tell me to stop
But I haven't had enough
If I'm still standing here
The words haven't cut deep enough
So I sharpen my tongue and repeat
All the things I deserve and hate about me
Until ulcers form in my stomach
And bile fills my throat, choking me
Then settle into the illness
A stomachache I suffer with daily
An inner conversation that makes me sick
I am just a very lonely girl
Vomiting instead of speaking up

DEPRESSION IS AN INFLICTION

Depression is an infliction I can't escape
It follows me like a ride I can't get off
Up and down, down and up,
It's an endless cycle
Where I can never be fully
One thing or the other
I get better, to get worse,
And get worse to get better

Depression haunts my every move
It's a poker game I can't win,
I can't get the upper hand
Just chasing the misery around
I finally feel free of it just to sink again
I can't get off this merry go round
It just keeps spinning
Around and around, I go,
Between happy and sad

Depression is all I can count on
It's the one thing I know better
Than the back of my hand
It's always been there for me
When things get worse
Or when things get better
It lurks in the corners
Waiting to strike me back
Down again

FEELS LIKE

The misery feels like a noose
Tied too tightly around my neck
I used to try to enjoy it
Like a sex act, seeking pleasure from it
But the tears always sting my eyes
And choking for air isn't sexy
When you just want it to kill you

The darkness feels like a blanket
Wrapped tightly around my body
I enjoy the warmth most the time
Like an embrace, holding me close
But the heat begins to burn my skin
And being on fire really hurts
When it won't let you die

The pain feels heavy like a gun
Pressed tightly to my head
I like the odds being against me
Like a bad bet going wrong
But the trigger is never pulled
And waiting for it to go off sucks
When you know death isn't following

CURSED

It's a weight around my neck
The whole world is pulling me down
Gravity has been an enemy
For as long as I've been alive
Flying was my destiny but
I was born in the wrong body
Cursed from the beginning
And nowhere feels like home
When you aren't in the right shell
My flesh and bones aren't my own
Mistakes happen, and I am one of them
Can't make something when I'm nothing
Just an error in the system
I never had a chance to be anything
Cursed from the very start
Doomed just to exist

WORSE

The worst is about to come
That's the fear that haunts me
When things get good
I freeze in terror
Because the bad is always
Right around the corner
It's how it's always been
And will always be
The bad isn't as bad as it could be
That's comforting to some
But to me it feels like
I'm taunting the Gods
When things get bad
I brace myself
Because I know bad things
Can only get worse
It's how it always happens
And it will happen again
I'm cursed to never enjoy the good
Because I know
It always gets worse

BITTER IRONY

It's a nagging feeling
On the back of my spine
A fuse that never blows
Just burns and burns
Traveling through my limbs
Waiting to explode
To turn my soul to shattered
Ashes of dreams that have died
I'm left for dead trying
To escape the suffering
My mortal enemy has
Always been myself
So I picked better weapons
Razorblades didn't cut it
Drugs didn't help it
So I picked harsher measures
And now we are here,
The time finally upon me
A plead on deaf ears
Begging for a better ending
But I sealed my fate
A very long time ago
No choice left for me
But to let it all play out
It haunts my head
Like a black hole
Waiting, wanting
Desiring to hurt me most
When I'm not ready for it
But the truth is

I'm always expecting it
Like bitter irony
Can't escape it
Can't embrace it
Can't have it
Just more anxiety
Consuming me whole

LIGHT VS DARK

There is a battle going on behind my eyes
A war that has been raging my whole life

The despair desperately wants to claim my soul
The hope dims every day but I grasp onto it

I feel myself sinking into the darkness
The ground calls for my name and I fight

Sometimes I let myself drown in the sorrow
Give into the blade and spill my own blood

The hope brightens for just a moment
And I believe I can keep it glowing

Crawling my way back to its embrace
But the cycle will always repeat

I'm getting so tired of losing my mind
The agony gets stronger as I grow colder

I can only hope the dip into the shadows
Doesn't last forever this time

I'm not ready to give up
But the choice has never been mine

I'm just a passenger in this war
Between the darkness and the light
Where my soul hangs in the balance

UNDONE

There is a silence in the noise
A gasp in the space between words
A chaos that can be ignored
But when you embrace it
It becomes your pain
When you see the cracks
They can't be unseen
And you will be undone

IMMORTAL

I looked for muses in the shadows
Searched for stars in the sunlight
Blacked out for days
Hoping a drunken state
Could inspire me better
But just ending up tired
Popped a few pills
To get me closer to God
But only sunk lower

I danced with wolves in caves
Climbed the highest tree
For the best of views
Sold my soul for
A little peace and quiet
But could only hear
The growling of hell hounds
Offered my heart for
A choir of angels singing
But went deaf with the silence

I found the way
The truth and the light
Dined on the blood
And body of Jesus
Prayed for forgiveness
But ended up in
My own personal hell
Cause some things
Can't be washed away
But it was worth trying

I tried to end my life
Walked out of the fire
Still alive and breathing
Just to get struck by a train
But somehow even that
Wasn't enough to kill me
I may be immortal after all
Cause only the dead never die
So what does that say about me

MY ATMOSPHERE

The storm clouds no long roll in
They just loom up above my head
Rain is not in the forecast it a constant
And thunder booms, lightning strikes
So often I've become accustomed to it
Hurricane season is all year around here
Avalanches happen every day at noon
This weather has become my normal
Dark and cloudy skies, gloom and doom
It's just my atmosphere

MY MIND IS CONDEMNED

The paint is chipping off the walls of my mind
The flowers I planted are beginning to rot
There is dust on every single surface
There are cobwebs in the corner of every room
My mind is decaying, the floorboards are cracking
The ceiling starts to collapse, spiders rain down
I once tried to repair this house of mine
But there aren't enough nails in the world
That I could use to mend the broken pieces
No plaster could cover up the holes I made
There is nothing to do but let it be condemned
Time to take a wrecking ball to it
One final blow to bring down what still stands
Time to let it fall apart, become ruins
Maybe I could rebuild it all
But I'll probably just join the ash
Let myself finally give up on fixing my mind
Time to accept that my mind is past repair
I have to let go any hope it can be saved
This house is not a home anymore
My mind becomes unlivable
Just like me

MY HEART IS BROKEN

The current knocks me back
I should be used to the rise of the tide
But the waves remain foes
I can't tame the sea I cried
My pain has grown out of control

The mountain overshadows me
I should know the way around
But the only way I know is through
I can't climb the dirt I dug up
My problems have piled too high

The sky darkens over my head
I should know how to see in it
But the light inside me has dimmed
I can't find my way out
My suffering is consuming

The life I made has shattered
I should know how put it back together
But the cracks are too small
I can't gather all the parts
My heart is beyond repair

MY BODY IS HAUNTED

Spiders fill both my lungs
I feel them with every breath I breathe
A heavy ache in every word I speak
An agony I can't outrun

Cobwebs live in my nerves
I feel them with every touch
A layer of dust I can't sweep up
A hurt I can't walk away from

Ghosts make a home in my heart
I feel them in every single vein
A brokenness I can't heal
An anguish I can't chase away

Death rattles in my bones
I feel it with every step I take
An ache in every movement
A pain I can't escape

NOT MADE FOR THIS WORLD

There is a crack in my brain
Where all my dreams seep through
And I've lost my way so many times
But it still hurts wandering aimlessly
My purpose died the first time
I tried to end everything
And I know now
I'll never get it back

There is nothing but ruins in my chest
Where all my love has turned to dust
And I've tried to keep some for myself
But the storms blew it all away
Scattering it among souls
Who give none of it back
I've been giving more
Than I take my whole life
And I understand now
That's on me

There is a hole in my soul
Where I've been trapped
For my entire lifetime
And I keep trying to crawl out
But there is no escaping the darkness
It's been consuming me since birth
Snuffing the light from my hands
And I think I finally accept that
I'm not made for this world

PERPETUAL DARKNESS

A fire has been dwindling in my core
Since I was three and reality became real
A snap to the present, a slip to the past
And I'm lost among the shadows
Taunting me with melancholy
Begging me to fade to black with them
But the edge of reason keeps me frozen
Even as insanity lingers ahead
I know better than to leap to the end
Not yet. Not now. Not until...

A sense of doom has been building inside me
Since I got my first glimpse of death
A dog's passing, cementing permeance is a lie
And I no longer saw a reason to try
When everything is going to stop
Why bother with the fundamentals of life
But the unknown keeps me going
I don't want to go to the other side
Not yet. Not now. Not until...

An evil has been set out to get to me
Since the day I was conceived
A family tree, or maybe a burning bush
And I will never know which one to believe
Laughter echoes among the screams
Tears fill the tub, blood stains and scars join
But I know how it goes right?
Across the street not down it
Not yet. Not now. Not until...

A peace has never been within my reach
Since I settled into the world around me
A single memory starts my descent
And I don't think it was anyone's fault
The lights just never fully turned on for me
Trapping me in perpetual darkness
But that was always hard to accept
Until now

INTO THE UNKNOWN

Staring into the unknown
I question every I have
Did I deserve it?
The good, the bad, all of it
What's ahead is a secret
And secrets scare me
When so much of the present
Is unknown as well
I guess I'll never know
The plan and how much of it
Was just me making
A mess of things

FUTURE RAINCLOUD

The time drags on in the heat of summer
Setting myself a blazed is always easy
When the cooler nights come in
I drown under a sea of blankets
Waiting for the sun to set on me
The dark sky reminds me I'm all alone
Even with a warm body next to me
I've flew too close to a black hole
Now it's pulling me into its orbit
And seasons come and go
While I wait for it to consume me
Because I'm just a dark cloud
In a clear blue summer sky
Nonexistent but still coming
As time rolls by, I know one day
I'll be the raincloud of winter
Ruining everything

DUST STORM

I choke on the dust of the chaos
The broken rumble surrounds me
I tore down the walls that held me in
But I released a monster instead
And there is no going back
The flood gates are open
And I'm vulnerable once again
The sun doesn't shine where I stand
I thought it was freedom
But it's just another cage
And I can't escape the damage I've done
Or pay back the debt I'm in
I struggle to accept my place
The throne is a glass house
The crown is made of thorns
And this kingdom is just ruins
So I run from it again
I recused myself from hell
Just to find myself in a new one
I refuse to let this wasteland be my tomb
But maybe what's best for me is
Being swallowed by the dust storm

FAKE ALIBI

I lie when I tell everyone I'm fine
And everybody knows it
They see the lack of light behind my eyes
No one can pinpoint why I am like this
I have an airtight alibi on why I won't die
And they all pretend to buy it
They'll act surprise when I do it
No one will be able to accuse them of faking
Until then we go on like everything is okay
And there are no warning signs
So they don't have to try to rescue me
Not that I'd let them anyways

NEVER WHOLE

I don't think I've ever been whole
Missing parts from the start
I gathered rumble and ruins
As I crawl through the darkness
Using duct tape and super glue
To patch up holes in my soul
But I know I'll never be whole

I don't think I'll ever be complete
Pieces began rotting early on
I tried to clean out the mold
As I swam in the sea of sorrow
Wadding knee deep in my tears
But I can't never be complete

I don't think I'll ever be saved
Cracks formed in my heart
I covered up the pain
As I faked happy at home
Pretending I knew what it meant
To smile without hurting
But I can never be saved

PLEASE DON'T

Don't tell me what to do
I never listen to reason
We all know that

Don't try and talk me down
I've never been worth saving
We can't deny that

Don't ask me why I'm like this
I don't have the answers
We should've known

Don't beg me to stay
I try not to make promises
We know I'll break

HOW...?

How am I supposed to keep going
When the hole in my chest keeps growing

How must I weather the storm
When it's been raging my whole life

How can I overcome the odds
When I keep making bad bets

How do I survive this
When it's killing me

How will I die
When I try to

How does it end
When I finally do it

I AM IT

If there was a chance
I blew it

If there was a way out
I passed it

If there was another option
I missed it

If there was anyone who cared
I ignored it

If there was hope
I lost it

If there was a way to save myself
I refused it

If there was a way to end this
I tried it

If there is someone to blame
I am it

ACCIDENTAL OVERDOSE

It's not everything I wanted
But it will do in a pinch
Plastering band aids on bullet holes

Using dialysis to clean my bloodstream
But you took root in my organs
No amount of detoxing can fix me

Unplug me, I don't want to be a vegetable
I'm brain dead since I let you in
Thinking you'd be enough for now
But somehow you because fatal

A cancer, spread throughout my body
Cut out this tumor
It's killing me

Suddenly I spike a fever I can't fight
You are an infection no antibiotics can cure
Poison with no antidote
No antidepressants to save me

I'm shackled to this hospital bed
As they operate on me without anesthesia
So I feel every cut
But you hide in my bones

Like growing pains, I feel you mainly at night
Restless leg syndrome urging me to move
But I can't escape the ache you cause me
I'm helpless to this disease
No doctor can heal me

You were supposed to be a one time drug
A painkiller, but now I'm addicted
You are my opioid
That's going to be the death of me
An accidental overdose

YOU'RE TOO LATE

Walls mile thick close off my soul
Keeping me locked in with demons
That I stopped fighting years ago
Because I know they will win in the end
And you will never see the worst of it
I only let you peek inside the room
So the darkness doesn't consume you too

Stones bounce off my glass windows
Nothing can break through them
The glass became bulletproof a long time ago
Nothing can ever hurt me like my own words
So every word you ever spoke get drowned out
By the sound of my own screams
Nothing you said will ever get through to me

My heart hangs from roots of a dying tree
Dangling underneath six feet of dirt
With no sunshine to help it grow
A seed I planted in hopes of finding you
But the drought came before you could
Rotting me to my core, killing all hope
That I could be someone worthy of your love

A bitter tang lingers on the tip of my tongue
The poison I leak could break an angel's wings
And it will do worse to you, my soul mate
The irony of finding the one you belong to
Long after you stopped breathing to live
Is knowing what could've been will never be
Because I'm too broken to be yours

It's too late for your love to save me
It's too late for us

I SIT

I sit
And wait for the feelings
To overwhelm me

I sit
And picture sharp objects
Slicing through skin

I sit
And imagine the blood
Spilling from my flesh

I sit
And don't dare to move for surely
I will do it

I sit
And try to push the thoughts
Out of my mind

I sit
And cry because why
Can't I not want to die

WEAK

I chalk it all up to bad luck
I ramble on about how I'm cursed
How the devil has it out for me
But I never mention how I am to blame
For every bad thing to happen to me
We can trace it back years
When I once knelt and prayed
But not to be healed or saved
I begged for death
I practiced tying a noose
Swallowing pill after pill
Cutting into my own flesh
Because I never wanted
To try and get better
I never tried to fix the mess
I only wanted it to end
Because I've always been
Weak

A LIFE OF WASTE

I have known for most my life
That my mind wasn't quite right
I was in the third grade
Weeding through the dirt
For pieces of glass
I was craving death, before I knew
Just how permanent it really was
My mind expanded, faster than my legs
I aged ten years, in 12 months
I was going insane, but couldn't name it
I was broken, before I was whole
And you can't fix something
When you're missing half the pieces
I was doomed and mentally ill
Before I was mentally developed
As close to pathetic as you can get
I was set up to fail
Even if the chips had aligned
Even if my childhood was better
I was always going to struggle
I was always going to drown
In all of my feelings
Some people are just born depressed
Some people are just born to die
And I was just born to waste time

TIME DOESN'T HEAL ALL THINGS

No amount of time will remove the scars
Even if the flesh heals over the years
The marks stick to my soul

No matter the time that passes me by
There will always be a hole inside my heart
It grows as I do

No number of good days can heal me
The happiness doesn't outweigh the pain
Tears are heavier than smiling

Not a thing can change the damage done
Nothing will ever fix me up enough
To no longer feel like dying

MY FATE IS DEPRESSING

My head is spinning
I'm at war once again
Picking different sides each day
Because I fear my time is coming
I've fought so hard to get here
Overcame my demons
But it is not enough to keep me
I've been pushing daisies for a lifetime
A change of scenery doesn't fix that
I was on borrowed time my whole life
Just a rotting corpse fighting back
Against the only outcome I ever had
Depression was always going to get me

PANDORA'S BOX OF DEATH

I opened pandora's box years ago
I don't remember when exactly
But I was younger than you'd expect

Searching playgrounds for glass
Something to make me bleed
To make the flesh match the soul

It was a taste of things to come
But even I didn't know it then
Couldn't see the future coming

I thought about it for years
Toyed with the key
But put off turning it

Until the night I gave in
Tempted into release
Not knowing what I did

Swallowing pill after pill
Until sweet sleep came for me
Waking up to misery

Still not realizing what I had done
Not accepting defeat meant
Releasing a new kind of suffering

Death now lurked all around me
Waiting, taunting, teasing
Because I asked for it

Opened the box
Tried it on
And now I'm stuck

Wearing scars of failure
Still wanting it
But never having it

Once you open Pandora's Box
It can never be sealed shut

Once you try to die
It's all you ever want

SELF DESTROYED

Is this how my world finally ends?
The ruins overturned the marble pathways
I've struck the match after draining the dams
Every mistake compacted into each other
The last stoned cast was by own hand
And I should've seen it coming
I placed my bet so long ago, but I forgot
Knew since I was three, I'd be my own downfall
Called my shot, and took the aim
Regret is an immense feeling
Now that I get to watch it happening
This is not what I really wanted
But the bill came due, and I went bankrupted
Trying to pay for my palace with blood
But there is never enough to shed
Without killing myself, so I did it
I built myself a tomb, and a crown of ivy
Bricked myself in to avoid the blast
Because I will walk out of this alive
But with everything I loved
Destroyed.

LIKE SAND THROUGH THE HOURGLASS...

I wasted my whole life in demise
I spent too much time fighting
Didn't notice myself aging

I thought I'd be dead by now
I planned it all out countless times
Didn't see the years passing

I found a way to hide within myself
I kept my secrets to myself
Didn't know time was slipping away

I figured I had more time
I used minutes as currency
Didn't realize hourglass was draining

A MISTAKE WAS MADE

I have carved out a hole in the shadows
A place for me to curl up and wait
For the ending to come for me
For death to finally take me

I tempted the wolves with my bloody wrists
A million times I let them feed on me
For a chance to end my misery
For nothing more than some peace

I made the bed nightmares haunt me in
A hard place to lay on a rock to comfort me
For there is nothing good coming
For I have lost all hope

I entered this hell of my free will
A mistake I can't undo for the life of me
For there is no going back
For I sealed my fate long ago

LITTLE MONSTER

I feel it eating away at my spine
A little parasite lives in my head
And it is moving its way through my body
Destroying all my sanity
Warping all my memories

I feel like I've become a host
A little insect lives in my blood stream
And it flows through my heart
Beating away at my hope
Tainting my dreams

I feel I lost control of myself
A little creature has taken over
And it pulls at the strings
Breaking everything I built
Hurting everyone I love

Now I feel nothing at all
A little monster has killed me
And as I lay in my flesh tomb
All I can do is watch as it
Fucks up my whole life

I HAVE A DEBT TO PAY

A terror makes a shiver run down my spine
I've gone too far into the darkness
The monsters that lie here want my blood
And I can't make enough to fend them off
I always knew it was going to end badly
But didn't think it would be like this

In the shadows they haunt me
My fears are starving
Ready to feast on what little hope I have left
I'm depleted, a void full of numbness
But they want to rip the shell apart
Revenge in any form is still payback
The the bill has come due
But I can't afford it

I pushed them down, let them rot
And they didn't forget
All the problems I shoved under the rug
Reappeared when the deal fell through
When I couldn't hold up my end
A bargain made of desperation
That I never thought I'd have to face
But I asked for peace
Got it for a moment
Not long enough to fix my soul
But still I felt it

The promise was fulfilled
And regardless of satisfaction
I have to pay for it now
But I'm too broken to do so
They set out to finish the job
The late fees have added up
Now I have debt to settle
A gift I once begged for
I now can't avoid
My death I have promised them
My soul theirs to collect

ALWAYS READ THE FINE PRINT

Every ounce of me is bruised
Only they aren't black and blue
You can't see them
But I can barely feel them
They are beneath the surface
Hidden in my bones
Inside the marrow

My wrists are covered in scars
Only the deep ones remain
You can see them up close
I don't try to hide them
They are reminder of the times
I bled for a sign of life
Hidden in my veins
In my heartbeat

The body I was born in carries a toll
Only I can't pay for it
A crumbling debt
You can loan me the currency
But I will never repay it
The interest rate is high
Hidden in the fine print
A form I signed without reading

EARTH IS CALLING

I feel the earth pulling me down
The dirt is trying to call me home
But I don't want to go back in the hole
Every time I sink a litter deeper
And crawling back out gets a little harder
Trying to keep my head in the clouds
Because up there I'm untouchable
Gravity always comes back for me
Setting me on the ground
That turns into quicksand
And it tries to consume me
Trap me under the surface
A dirt coffin to contain my soul
Because it's been waiting for me since 13
I offered the earth my corpses
And have yet to deliver
But it won't let me forget my debt
It keeps calling me

DEATH KNOWS ME

The pressure presses down on me
My heels dig into the shallow grave
There is dirt under my fingernails
Death beckons me, calling me by name

The toll has been taken out on my flesh
My scars light up in the darkness around me
There is blood dripping down my arms
Death embraces me, he knows me by name

The life has been sucked from my lungs
My heart is no longer beating
There is a beauty in dying
Death greets me, he knows me by name

Death welcomes me in
He greets me like an old friend
Cause he's known me for awhile
He knows my name

WALTZ WITH THE DEVIL

We dance the waltz and tango
Entwined, our bodies sway back and forth
To the tempo played for us
I watch your feet gracefully
Aware I'm out matched
You dip me back, and I pray you drop me
But you are a master of this art
You lead me across the ballroom floor
I try to avoid stomping on your feet
As mine ache in four inches heels a size too small
The music switches from upbeat to somber
But you don't let me go, you grip me tighter
And I know this dance only ends
When you are finished with me
There are no other partners to cut in
No one to save me from this dance
My feet may bleed, but you still spin me
I should've known better
Than to dance with the Devil
Here in a hell where the party
Never ends and I can't escape

DEFEATED

Defeat came for me

I fought with all I had
Every ounce of my blood
Stains the battle ground
I poured my heart and soul
Into the gun powder

Every bullet I shot
Took part of me with it
But still it wasn't enough
I always knew it
But still sent out my spirit
To fight alongside of me

I tried to out stand my foes
I threw grenades of my hate
But they never went off
I've never hated anymore
More than myself
So, they just sat in my fields
Waiting for me to walk on them

I was not a brave solider
I tried to hide out, take cover
Didn't believe in friendly fire
But found out all the weapons
Were aimed at myself

My army deserted me
I was alone wolf in a nuclear war
Brought old age weapons
They had weapons of mass destruction
So I had no chance and no choice
Surrendering was a death sentence

I knew I lost either way
And the final strike
Came from my own hand
So, my enemies get no glory
But I still lose everything
Still defeated

SUCCUMB

The hope dims
The darkness fades in
All around me
I've stood here before
And I know I will again
Even when the sun comes
Shining once again
I always get back here
I always end up
In this black place
But what if I don't
Try to get out of it
And just let myself
Succumb to it?

FIELD OF TRAGEDY

My mind is a giant field of landmines
It's been infected for as long as I can remember
Tainted with memories that cut like barbwire
Or the glass I searched for on playgrounds
Before I should've know what it meant
To want to hurt on the outside like I did within
I was just a child, sick with unnamed inflictions
That would haunt me through the years
Holding me back, drowning my ambitions
Because I could never get far enough away from
The demons hunting me in forms of people who
Swore they would never hurt me, but always did
And I can never get back the time I wasted
And I don't even want to erase the memories
They keep my company in my field of tragedy
Where I wait for the earth to swallow me whole
Because I am never going to be happy, not truly
That is an impossible task since my heart broke
From my own hands, I've been the best enemy
The biggest foe I ever had was my reflection
I've been the largest predator, out to get myself
It's been a long road to end up here though
In a field of ruins, and the bombs will explode
But only when I don't want them to, like irony
I've always been sick, but not bad enough
For it to actually kill me, just to tease me
With the promise of release
But this field won't let me go
And all I can do it sit, and wait
For the ending

ALL TOO SLOWLY

This pain is phantom
But my nervous system
Feels every ounce of it

I can't push forward
And I can't go backwards
I'm in limbo. Purgatory

And the flags go up
Red and white
My cry for help

Because my mouth can't
Form the words
But surely, they all know

I'm stuck here in the darkness
No light gets in. No hope
But not hopeless

Please someone know
Please help me
Someone save me
Do something

I'm dying
All too slowly

I HATE IT HERE

Memories flash behind my eyes
A blackhole swirls inside my mind
Sucking me deeper into the dark
I hate it here

Tears from behind my eyes
A well overfills inside my mind
Drowning me in the darkness
I hate it here

Pain turns to blood in front of my eyes
A scream echoes inside my mind
Tempting me deeper into the dark
I hate it here

THE WELL

I'm stuck in a well of constant despair
The walls echo with memories
I really don't want to recall
Remains of the girl I was meant to be
Keeps me company in the dark
And I'm not sure how I got down here
But there is no way to get out

THE VOID

Inside me in a pit of darkness
I fall into it, time and time again
Getting lost in the blackness
All light gets smothered by it
All hope dies within it

Inside me is a brick wall
I run into it, over and over again
Hitting my head against the stone
Everything hurled at it breaks
Everything I need is on the other side

Inside me is a well of hope
I try to drink from it, again
But nothing remains inside of it
All I had is evaporated.
Everything it held, dried up

Inside of me is a void
I sit inside it, once again
Letting myself disappear
Nothing can save me from it
Nothing can pull me out

WHO'S REALLY TO BLAME

How many years did I
Blow out my birthday candles
Wishing for something
To end my existence and suffering?
More than I can count with both hands
But I could never blow them
Out with one breath
So maybe that's why
They went unanswered

I've seen more than
My fair share of shooting stars
Closing my eyes
Hoping their dying light
Would grant me my wish to join them
But they have their own demises to face
So they couldn't help me with mine

I knelt down many times
Praying to be set free
Asking for salvation
In the form of an early grave
But the man in the sky
Has more pressing things
I suppose a broken soul
Like me is just a lost cause
Begging to die when
The whole world is ablaze is selfish

When I took matters into my own hands
With pills, blades and drugs I realized
I can't point fingers at candles, stars or God
When not even I can stop the hurting
I guess I was just born to live in agony

BUT MYSELF

Call the morgue
All my dreams are dead
I grieve for them still
But I nailed the coffin shut
Got no one to blame
For how everything ended
But myself

Call the cemetery
All the parts of me I liked
Are hanging from the branches
And I tied the noose
It's no use pointing fingers
At anyone else
But myself

Call upon death
All that is left of me
Is no longer safe
And I got no one to hide from
Not anyone else
But myself

THE PROBLEM INCREASES

Sorrow no longer flows through my soul
It has made a permanent home inside me

Pain no longer throbs throughout my body
It has become a constant feeling within me

Sadness no longer weights me down daily
It is now consuming me from the inside out

THE WEIGHT IS CRUSHING

I collapse into it
Crumbling to ruins
I am not going to make it
Through this time
My eyes begin to sting
I fight against the tears
But fall to pieces regardless
I am not going to make it
Through this time
The pain is overwhelming
I give up on trying
Cutting into my skin
I am not going to make it
Through this time
My heart is shattering
I surrender to the sadness
No use trying anymore
I am not going to make it
Through this time

HERE LIES THE QUESTIONS

How did I get here?
Countless wrong turns
On a bad path

What did I do here?
Bad bets in a long game
Rigged from the start

Why did I stay here?
Everywhere else just
Brought me back here

NEVER GETTING BETTER

I am never getting better
The sentiment is lost on them
The facts are hard to face
And the the truth hurts
When they won't let go
But I am never getting better

I am never getting better
The burden is heavy to carry
The goodbye will be awful
And the ending rough
When they won't accept it
But I am never getting better

I am never getting better
They can't believe it
They won't listen to reason
And they can't see
When I'm suffering
Because I am never
Getting better

SCARRED

I stare at the last little scar on my arm
All the others have faded away
All that remains of my past
Coping mechanisms, have healed
I wish I could say I'm glad
I wish I felt better
But the marks can fade from my flesh
But the pain always remains
I could never cut it away
I could never bleed it out
Until my dying day, I will feel it
All the pain I've endured
Left a fatal wound on my soul
For all my days, I will be broken
My arms don't look marred anymore
But my heart still is
But my soul still hurts
I am still broken
I am still scarred

BROKEN GIRL

Feel myself slipping again
Holding on tightly to myself
But I seep through my fingertips
Dripping on the floor of regret
I don't know why I always end up
Back to this point

How long do I have to suffer for my sins
Why am I stuck in this vicious cycle
Did I not pay back my debts
I tried to change it one too many times
But I accepted my fate and was still denied

Too much sadness consumed me
I fall to the waste side over and over
Having to climb my way back
Just to have the rug pulled from under me

This isn't fair, and I know that
But it is what it is and I'm no more than
The fracture pieces of a broken girl
Slipping to the darkness once more

SOUL OF THESEUS

I have reinvented myself countless times
Changes around my organs like a surgeon
Rewiring my brain, restarting the game
Hoping I'd find a form that wouldn't hurt
But you can change all the parts
Can rearrange the placement
But the soul is still the same
Still broken

THE GIRL IN THE VOID

No one believes me
The girl who called wolf
About a dozen times
And that's just the tries
They all know about
But there were plenty more

No one understands me
The girl who fell down
A hundred times now
And that's just the times
They were there to see it
But there were so many more

No one knows me
The girl in the void
Wasting away in hell
And that's a secret
They don't know
But there are more

THE WELL DRIED UP

Is this the best I can do?
I swear I thought I had more to offer
I thought I was stronger than this
But I feel like I've given all I can give
And it's not enough
To get me further than this
I'm at the end of my rope
This is the best I can do
And it will never be better than this
All I have is deep seated regret
All the strength I wasted
All the things I accomplished
For everyone but myself
What a fool I was
To let them have all of that
But I can't take it back
If I could I still wouldn't
Because I have nothing left now
The well has ran dry
The ink dried up
I have no more left to give
My best has come and went away
And this will never be okay
This is the end of the road for me
The best I can do is not enough
I was never good enough

FATHOMS DEEP

The pain has seeped into my marrow
Like lead in my bones, it pulls me under
The currents are pulling me down
And I can't come back up to breathe again
The misery has a death grip on my legs
An anchor made of every bad mistake
I'm sinking to the bottom with no hope
Because the sadness is in my soul
A wide-open hole, flooding with salt water
Making all the wounds burn even more
I don't think I'll make it to land again
Becoming one with the deep blue sea
Nothing more than another shipwreck
Forgotten, like all the sailors before
I wasn't even a captain, but I sank with it
A vessel of broken cargo on the ocean floor
History that no one cares to find
Depths no one will explore
I am ruins, left to rust fathoms deep

NOT THROUGH

The weight is crushing
I collapse into it
Crumbling to ruins
I am not going to make it
Through this time

My eyes begin to sting
I fight against the tears
But fall to pieces regardless
I am not going to make it
Through this time

The pain is overwhelming
I give up on trying
Cutting into my skin
I am not going to make it
Through this time

My heart is shattering
I surrender to the sadness
No use trying anymore
I am not going to make it
Through this time

ENOUGH

I've fallen down again
Settled into the dirt
Let the lights dim
Don't make me
Get back up
This time

I've had enough

ANYMORE

I will not cry
The tear wont form
And I will not yell
My lips wont part
But above all else
I will not love
Cause my heart
Won't beat
Anymore

A CYCLE OF DARKNESS

I settle into the darkness
Make my home with the corpses
Of every me I've ever slaughtered
The ghosts refuse to speak to me
I ruined their lives, and they mine
But I deserve it, they know that
And I know they deserve it too

Nothing makes sense in darkness
A home built on broken promises
The vows we made in the mirror
"You will be better this time"
"You won't destroy it again"
But they were lies, we all knew it
And yet we believed them still

The darkness is all around us
A graveyard of all our memories
All the hopes and dreams and tears
Collected like haunted trophies
We can't escape out failures
But we pass the blames around
And the next one takes over
Until the darkness collects them too

A PLAGUE

Life has me in chokehold
It keeps me in place
Growth isn't an option for me
I made my peace
I made my plan
Now good things avoid me
Like I'm a plague wrapped
In death's embrace

SLIPPING INTO INSANITY

I am miserable
The pain hurts too much
The hurt drives me crazy

I am terrible
The bad words fly from me
The fly must die somehow

I am starving
The food doesn't taste right
The taste is poisoning me

I am desperate
The need gnaws at me all night
The night is growing bright

And I am a mess
The dirt sticks to my flesh
The flesh can never be clean enough

And I am losing it
The bad thoughts wander aimlessly
The thoughts overwhelm me

I am broken
The pieces can't be put back together
The togetherness is too much

I am done
The insanity must end
The end comes for me

And I am no more

YOU JUST LOST THE GAME

If you ask me on a good day
I will confess it with a laugh
If you ask me on bad day
I will deny it to your face
But if you ask me on my worst day
I will tell you right out
I'm going to kill myself

If you beg me not to on a good day
I will tell you I make no promises
If you beg me not to on a bad day
I will swear it's not my plan
If you beg me not to on the greatest day of my life
I will confess that's it no longer up to me
I'm going to kill myself

If you ask me why on a good day
I may just tell you every reason
If you ask me why on a bad day
I will probably say I don't know
If you ask me why on the worst day
I promise you don't want to know what I will say
I'm going to kill myself

If you wonder if a good day will stop me,
It will
If you wonder if a bad day will make me
It might
If you wonder if a great day will keep me
You are wrong
I'm going to kill myself

THE UGLIEST HOUSE ON THE STREET

I suppose the writing was on the wall
The foundation was cracked from the start
Windows nailed shut should've been a sign
The way cobwebs hugged every corner
And bugs crawled on the hardwood floor
All telling signs of the things to come
But we ignored them, you and I, and them

Everyone who's eyes fall on me pretends
They don't notice the red flashing lights
Ignores the darkness of every room
And the way my laugh echoes down halls
The red paint running down the walls
Because who has the time to address that
Or even knows how to fix it
Certainly not them, me, nor you

So best to gloss over the cold hard facts
Dust and sweep, put down a rug
Hang up a few picture frames
Anything to cover up the problems
But when this house crumbles
Taking me down with it
Who will be surprised
Not you, not them, and not me

DEAD

Deadlocked
The whole world stalls
Sand through the hourglass
Doesn't fall at this moment
I have a choice to make

Deadpan
The reality sets in
My heart in my chest
Refuses to beat anymore
I have no more time left

Dead
The decision is made
My life shatters to pieces
No longer my own
I have given up

MY WORLD ENDS

My world is going to cave in
Everything is on fire all around me
I have burnt it all down once again
Ripped myself to shreds
Like I've been doing since I was a kid

My world is going to stop
Everything is crumbing to dust
I wrecked the life I built once more
Cut myself into pieces
Like I've been doing my whole life

My world is coming to an end
Everything always does
I make sure of it
Killing myself
Like I've been trying to do
Always

WELL TRAVELED

The water is steady, but my feet are heavy
I can barely swim, so I float far away
The shore drifts out of my eyesight
The tide has carried me away again

The forest is vast and I'm just so tiny
I can barely see, so I sit against a tree
The night comes to black out my sight
The wild has claimed me once more

The mountain is steep but I'm clumsy
I can barely find my footing, so I trip
The fall knocks me out, my vision blurs
The altitude has made me sick again

The road is long and I'm very tired
I can barely keep up, so I stop trying
The map falls from my hand, I am lost
The journey has ended for me
Finally

I SUPPOSE THIS IS IT

I suppose they need me to point
To draw a map to the moment
Connect the dots, underline it
So they can understand why I did it

I suppose they want to pretend
That there weren't warning signs
No alarm bells tolling or flashing lights
So they can sleep better at night

I suppose I should leave behind
Something to comfort them
A peace offering, a goodbye note
So they know I don't blame them

So here we go...

YOU COULD NOT

I felt joy when you found me
It brought me peace for a moment
But a moment is not enough to free me
From the burdens I'm carrying
You could not save me
You could not stop me

I saw the light behind your eyes
I felt the warmth radiating from your soul
But it isn't enough to thaw my heart
Or enough to keep it beating steadily
You could not save me
You could not stop me

I knew you were my soulmate from that day
I felt the instant connect and chemistry
But unfortunately for us both I sold my soul
So long ago, there is no way to ask for it back
You could not save me
You could not stop me

And I know it will destroy you
I can feel your future pain
But even that is not enough to keep me
I am too far gone to be fixed
You could not save me
You could not stop me

BAD AT GOODBYES

How do I say goodbye?
Whisper to you as you sleep
Knowing you won't hear it
Hoping it seeps in through your dreams

How do I say goodbye?
Squeezing your hand as we walk together
Knowing you don't know morse code
But still hoping you understand it

How do I say goodbye?
Fighting back tears as you kiss my lips
Knowing you can't feel me slipping away
Hoping you'll forgive me in the end

How do I say goodbye?
Leaving behind a file of notes
Knowing it won't make any sense to you
But hoping you find peace in them

How do I say goodbye?
Saying the word is not enough
Knowing you'll find me dead
Hoping I'm not

THEIR GRIEF WILL BE TEMPORARY

They are going to hate me
Burying me six feet below
The feet they used to walk
Beside me and my burdens

They are going to cry for me
Laying me to rest far a way
On the other side I longed for
As they held me too close

They are going to miss me
As their lives continue on
With me no longer there to
Bring them down anymore

They are going to let me go
Eventually
When they finally realize
This is what's best for me

SORRY

It hurts
I ache
It's too much
I am suffering

It stings
I cry
It's agony
I am exhausted

It burns
I lie
It's horrible
I am dying

It sucks
I plead
It's hell
I am sorry

DOOMSDAY CLOCK

The clock is racing
But I'm not trying
To outrun it anymore

The time is coming
And I can't tell them
Goodbye

The end is closing in
And I don't care
About what's ahead

The finale is here
But I won't cry
I'm ready to go

The alarm bells toll
And I'm aware
The end is here

IT ALL ENDS

Hopelessness settles into my bones
Like anchors pulling me down below
I know I have nothing left in me
The world dims, letting me know
This is the end, once more

Sadness evaporates from my body
But this is not a good sign to me
I know now, that nothing can hurt me more
As the world around me grows so cold
I accept this as the end, suddenly

Painful for just a moment, then no longer
The light behind my eyes goes out
I knew time was never on my side
But now my world is over
It all ends
Now

GRIEVING

If grief is the product of love
I will cut off the arteries to my heart
I never want to feel this pain again

If the first step is denial
I'll admit to all of it
I don't want to move forward

Acceptance comes in waves
So, I shove my hands in my pockets
No one will ever touch me again

If dying is just the end
I will spend the days of my life
Searching for the grim reaper

I won't say it
They can't make me
I won't say it
They can't make me

Throw open the casket
Put out this fire
I can't believe

This is goodbye

A LAST PARTING

So long,
My time has come
An ending I welcome

Farewell
My heartbeat ceases
And I feel peace

Goodbye,
My life ends
Finally

GOODBYE

AFTER THOUGHTS

If you read these poems and saw your own struggles in the words, let me tell you, it does actually get better, and it will get worse, but the sun always comes back around.

Do not give up.

Find a way to enjoy the good times, they will get you through the dark ones.

You are <u>not alone</u>. <u>Reach out</u>. <u>Get help</u>. <u>Be safe</u>.

Resources are available.

<u>Suicide Hotline: 988</u>

THANK YOU

As with all my books, they would not exist without my amazing husband, who pushes and pulls me through all my doubts. He supports me when I need it, and encourages me to keep going when I feel like giving up. *I love you, Matthew.*

To my family. We are all a little strange, and I'm so grateful that we are that way. Thank you for the endless support, love and care. I would not be who I am without you. *I love you all.*

To the people who continue to read my books, from the poetry books to the full length novels, your support means the world to me. I am grateful for each everyone of you. *Thank you.*

My fellow authors and writing community, I owe you the world. Your support is a debt I will never be able to repay. Thank you for the endless support and encouragement. *I appreciate you all so much.*

STAY STRONG.

ABOUT THE AUTHOR

Samantha Butterfield comes from the Bay Area, where she has lived her whole life. She has been writing stories and poems since she was young. Finding comfort in words, she loves crafts deep, emotional poetry or complex characters in drama filled worlds. Drawing from her own personal struggles she has put out a few poetry books, that touch on the hardships of mental illness. She doesn't stop at just poetry though, using her own emotions to create unique characters in her full-length novels as well.

She is currently working on an interconnected rockstar romance series along side her poetry. The first book, A Dark Melody is out now. She will be releasing more romance novels in 2026, so follow her on social media for more updates.

When she isn't writing, she fills her time reading with her lucky black cat, Hemingway curled in her lap and listening to music. Or playing games with her husband and friends.

Also by
Samantha Butterfield

depression: a book of poems

Step into the darkness beyond the depths of sadness in this collection of dark poems. Depression: a book of poems takes you to front line of an internal war. The words reflect on the battle in a haunting but elegant way. They weave the emotion of pain and suffering in each line.

Bleak Pages

In my darkest moment, poetry was how I expressed myself. These poems are my raw emotions on display, for the world to see. They are dark and gritty, sometimes grim, but writing them helped me get through the bleakness, and so I put them out to let other know, they are not alone. Even in the bleakest of times, there is always hope. There is always help.

A Dark Melody

Some melodies are light. Others are DARK.

Abbey Dark is the biggest female rockstar in the scene, but behind the sold-out shows, screaming fans, and bright lights, she is unraveling. At her breaking point from the pressures of fame, high expectations, and loneliness, Abbey is barely holding it together.

Enter Wesley Whitmore, the kind-hearted frontman of the band Haunting Memories. With a passion for music, a big heart, and eyes that see beyond the stage lights, Wes isn't just another opening act, on yet another long tour. He is the lifeline Abbey desperately needs.

www.ingramcontent.com/pod-product-compliance
Lightning Source LLC
Chambersburg PA
CBHW060154130626
46556CB00006B/2638